# Contents

# At Home in Freshwater

There is an amazing variety of plants and animals living in rivers and lakes, in spite of the challenges they face in these **biomes**. Steep mountain rivers have fast-moving water that can wash plants and animals away from their homes. There is less **oxygen** and light in deeper water, so living things have to find clever ways to get the air and light that they need to survive.

## Going With the Flow

Some river plants have leaves **adapted** to cope with the movement of river water. For example, some have feathery leaves that allow water to filter through without dragging the plants away. Others have long, narrow leaves that are very flexible. They follow the flow of the water rather than fighting against it.

# AT HOME IN THE BIOME

# RIVERS and LAKES

Louise and Richard Spilsbury

Published in paperback in 2017 by Wayland

Editor: Sarah Eason
Cover design: Lisa Peacock

Produced for Wayland by Calcium

Dewey Number: 577.6'3-dc23
ISBN: 978 0 7502 9760 8
10 9 8 7 6 5 4 3 2 1

Wayland
An imprint of
Hachette Children's Group
Part of Hodder & Stoughton
Carmelite House
50 Victoria Embankment
London EC4Y 0DZ

An Hachette UK Company
www.hachette.co.uk

www.hachettechildrens.co.uk

**Picture acknowledgements:**

Key: b=bottom, t=top, r=right, l=left, m=middle, bgd=background

Dreamstime: Flyfishingnation 15, Fotografescu 13, Holger Leyrer 9, Krzysztof Odziomek 12–13, Photographerlondon 25, Rdonar 10–11; Shutterstock: Jody Ann 1, 27, Ryan M. Bolton 16–17, Marek Cech 19, Strahil Dimitrov 28–29, Erni 11, guentermanaus 29, Horse Crazy 18–19, Kanokratnok 20–21, Elizaveta Kirina 21, Sergey Krasnoshchokov 24–25, Martin Maritz 23, Johannes Dag Mayer 26–27, Yakov Oskanov 22–23, M. Pellinni 4–5, Pi-Lens 8–9, Sekar B 14–15, siwasasil 7, Dave Strickland 17, topimages 5, Oleg Znamenskiy 6–7.

Algae are green, plant-like living things often seen on rocks near water or on the water's surface. Algae look slimy or sometimes stringy. Algae do not have leaves, stems, **roots** or flowers as plants do, but like plants they make their food using sunlight in a process called **photosynthesis**. By floating on the water's surface, algae get the light they need to make their food.

*These river plants spread out their feathery leaves to maximise the amount of light they receive.*

# Water Lilies

Giant water lilies have some of the biggest leaves in the world. Their huge leaves float on the surface of some of the world's rivers and lakes. They look like giant green plates!

## Reaching for the Light

The roots of water lilies grow into the muddy beds of lakes and ponds. Plants need water and air to grow, but they also need sunlight to make food by photosynthesis. Without it, plants die. Water lilies grow incredibly long stems that can reach up to 6 metres long, to hold their leaves up to the light at the water's surface. The leaves are flat and round, and have ribs, like spokes in a wheel. These support the weight of the leaves so they can float on the surface.

The underside of a giant water lily leaf has a lot of sharp spikes to stop fish from eating it!

HOME SWEET HOME

Giant water lily leaves can be up to 1.8 metres across, so they are quite heavy. To make sure they float well, they have spaces inside them that trap pockets of air. These work like flotation devices to keep the leaves floating on the water's surface.

# Diving Beetles

Great diving beetles are large beetles that spend most of their time diving underwater, just as their name suggests! These large, fearsome-looking beetles fly between ponds, scanning the water for the tadpoles, insects and tiny fish that they eat.

## Diving Down

A great diving beetle breathes through tiny holes in its stomach. At the surface of a pond, it pushes its stomach into the air and collects an air bubble. When it dives underwater, it breathes using the air from inside the air bubble, a little like the way human divers carry a tank of oxygen to breathe underwater. A diving beetle catches **prey** in its large jaws, then sucks it into its hungry mouth. When it runs out of air, it swims to the surface to take in more air so it can hunt again.

The diving beetle's body has a long, slim shape to help it cut quickly through the water as it dives for prey.

## HOME SWEET HOME

Female diving beetles cut holes in pond plant stems that grow above the water. They lay their eggs inside the holes. When diving beetle **larvae** hatch out, they cling to sticks or plants and eat prey that passes by.

# Crayfish

The American signal crayfish is a frightening freshwater **predator**. This large, lobster-like animal is found in slow-moving rivers and in lakes. It feeds on a variety of plants, fish, frogs and other animals, and it even eats other crayfish!

## Clawed Crayfish

The signal crayfish grows to about 8 centimetres long. It has two huge front claws, or pincers, which are used for catching prey and attacking predators. It also uses its pincers to bring the food it catches towards its mouth. The crayfish has four pairs of legs that allow it to walk across the riverbed. It also uses its legs to fan water towards its **gills** so it can breathe. If the crayfish needs to get somewhere quickly, it swishes its tail up and down to propel itself backwards in the water.

# HOME SWEET HOME

The signal crayfish mostly comes out at night. The rest of the time it takes shelter under rocks and stones on the riverbed. It can also shelter in holes among underwater tree roots, or in burrows and holes that it digs along the muddy riverbank.

The crayfish's hard, outer covering and its huge pincers make it a dangerous predator.

# Pike

Pike are predators that feed on fish and other animals in lakes and slow-moving rivers. These long, sleek fish can grow up to 1 metre long. They hide among the weeds at the side of rivers and dart out quickly to catch passing prey.

## Peeking Pike

The pike has large eyes high up on its head that it uses to look for prey in murky, weed-filled waters. When it spots a meal, the pike's large, powerful tail propels it forwards at impressive speeds. As it closes in on its prey, it opens its large mouth, which is full of sharp, pointed teeth. It uses its teeth to grab and hold on to the slippery fish it eats.

A pike can eat a prey animal of up to half its own body weight!

**HOME SWEET HOME**

The beautiful pattern of broken stripes along the pike's body provides it with **camouflage**. The markings are usually green and yellow, but the colour depends on where the pike lives. The markings make the pike so difficult to see among water weeds that other fish do not notice the pike waiting to ambush them.

# Salmon

Salmon are unusual river fish. Young salmon hatch from eggs in rivers, but as adults they live in the ocean. They may have to travel hundreds of kilometres between a river and the ocean, and face many predators along the way!

## Heading Home

When it is time to have their young, adult salmon swim from the areas of the ocean where they have been living and feeding to a river. Amazingly, they go back to the river they were born in by remembering the particular smell of that river! After **breeding**, some adult salmon are so exhausted from the trip that they die. The young salmon that hatch from eggs live for up to seven years in the river. They feed and grow until they are adults and ready to make the long journey to the ocean. This event is called the salmon **migration**.

## HOME SWEET HOME

When salmon migrate upriver they often have to leap over rocky waterfalls to reach the part of the river where they breed. Salmon are able to leap up to 3.7 metres at a time as they rush to the breeding ground.

Large, adult Atlantic salmon are usually silvery-grey with black spots to camouflage them in the water.

# Fish Eagles

Fish eagles are often seen perching on high branches that hang over a river or lake. They sit very still, their large eyes on the lookout for fish swimming in the water below. When they spot prey, they move in quickly for the kill.

## Swooping Low

African fish eagles have wide wings, which they use to swoop low over the water. When they reach their target, they bring both feet forward and grab hold of their prey with their long, powerful **talons**. When they catch a small fish, they carry it back to a tree to eat it. If they catch a fish that is too heavy to carry while they are flying, they drag it through the water to the edge of the river or lake, where they can eat their meal.

To get all the fish they need to survive, most African fish eagles only have to spend about 10 minutes a day hunting.

HOME SWEET HOME

The fish eagle has a sharp, curved beak. It uses this and its talons to hold its prey while it feeds. It also uses its beak to pull the **scales** off the fish and to tear its prey into small pieces that are easy to eat.

# Kingfishers

Kingfishers perch on plants at the river's edge to watch for prey. These birds can also flap their wings to hover just above the water's surface. They use their eyes to find fish, shrimp, tadpoles and other small prey, but, amazingly, they close their eyes to catch them!

## Dive and Spear

Once a kingfisher has spotted its prey and worked out how deep the animal is in the water, the acrobatic bird dives swiftly and accurately. As it enters the water, it opens its very long, sharp beak and closes its eyes. As it leaves the water with its catch in its dagger-like beak, it opens its eyes again and flies back to its perch. There it kills the prey by hitting it against a branch or firm stem.

## HOME SWEET HOME

Kingfishers make their nests in tunnels that they dig in the riverbank. The birds make a dip at the end of the tunnel to stop their eggs from rolling out. The parents have to work hard to feed the six or seven chicks that hatch out of the eggs. Each chick needs to eat about 15 fish every day!

Kingfishers need to eat their own body weight in fish each day.

# Giant Otters

Giant otters are also known as river wolves because they are such fearsome predators. As their name suggests, they are one of the largest otters in the world.

## Underwater Hunter

A giant otter eats mainly fish. It spots prey using its large eyes. Its whiskers also sense the ripples of water that fish create when they swim, which tells the otter where the fish are. To catch prey, a giant otter moves its large **webbed** feet and wide, flat tail to propel itself quickly through the water. It has a mouth full of razor-sharp teeth to catch and feed on its prey. The otter can stay underwater for up to eight minutes, and as it dives it closes its ears and nostrils to keep out water. Its soft, thick brown fur is waterproof and keeps it warm in deep, cold water.

*Giant otters eat mainly fish, but they also catch crabs, small alligators and even small anaconda snakes!*

## HOME SWEET HOME

Giant river otters live and raise their young in dens. They dig dens under fallen trees or on the riverbank. Family members mark the **territory** where they live and hunt with their droppings, and will attack other otters that enter their territory.

# Hippos

Hippopotamuses, or hippos, are enormous, barrel-shaped animals that live in shallow lakes and rivers in Africa. They usually spend the day lazing in the water and go in search of food as the sun sets. They walk a long way each night, looking for grass to eat.

## Graceful Giants

Hippos may be huge but they can swim and move very gracefully in water. A hippo's eyes and nose are high up on the top of its head. This allows the animal to breathe and keep a lookout for predators, such as crocodiles, when the rest of its bulky body is underwater. If a hippo sees a lion or other predator on land, it can run as fast as a human back to the water, where it is safer.

The hippo is the third-largest land mammal in the world. Despite being so large, hippos can move surprisingly quickly!

## HOME SWEET HOME

Hippos spend most of their daylight hours in water. They rest, play, squabble among themselves and **digest** their food for up to 16 hours a day. It gets very hot during the day in Africa, so staying in the water helps to keep the heavy hippos cool.

# Brown Bears

Every year, brown bears gather along rivers in places where salmon swim upstream to their breeding grounds. These large mammals come to the rivers to catch and eat salmon. The feast keeps the bears alive during the long winter months when food is scarce.

## Keeping Warm

A brown bear has thick fur and a layer of fat beneath its skin. This keeps it warm as it wades into cold mountain rivers to catch salmon. The bear eats huge amounts of food during the summer. By the autumn, it usually weighs twice as much as it did in the spring! Brown bears have to eat a lot because they **hibernate** inside the dens they dig in the ground during the winter. They live off the fat they stored in the summer until the spring comes.

**HOME SWEET HOME**

Brown bears catch fish from rivers in different ways. Some catch salmon in their mouths as the fish leap out of the water. Some bears dive underwater to grab their food. Others try to swat the salmon out of the water with one hard swipe of their huge paws. Mother bears bring their cubs to the river's edge to watch the adults catching salmon. This teaches the cubs how to hunt.

*Large male brown bears often compete for the best fishing spots along a river.*

# Beavers

Beavers are large rodents that chop down trees and branches to build giant homes, called lodges, in rivers and lakes. Large families of beavers live in these lodges, which can only be reached by underwater entrances.

## Busy Beavers

Beavers build a new lodge every autumn. They use their huge front teeth to chop down small trees and branches. They use their mouths to drag these into the water and stack them up to build the lodge. Then they line the entrance with grass and mud. Beavers keep warm and give birth to their young inside the lodges. They also escape there for safety from predators such as wolves. They even take some branches underwater as an emergency food supply, in case their pond freezes over in the winter and they get stuck inside the lodge!

Beavers use their sharp teeth to strip bark and leaves from trees for food. The tips of beaver teeth are worn down by gnawing, so they constantly regrow.

**HOME SWEET HOME**

Beavers can hold their breath for 15 minutes. They have transparent, or see-through, eyelids. This helps them to see underwater with their eyes closed. Beavers swim using their wide, flat tails. They also slap their tails on the water's surface to warn other beavers of nearby predators.

# Rivers and Lakes Under Threat

Rivers and lakes are amazing biomes full of fascinating wildlife, but some are under threat. Some rivers are damaged when pollution, such as factory waste or oil, runs into them. Wildlife is disturbed when people build along lakes and rivers, or drive fast boats across them. Wildlife is also affected when people take too many fish from rivers, leaving animals without food.

## Protecting Our Rivers and Lakes

People are helping river and lake biomes. They make laws to stop pollution and to limit the number of fish that can be caught. They create nature reserves or national parks, special areas of land that are protected by law. **Conservation** groups also raise money to help protect **endangered** animals, such as the pink river dolphin.

Pink river dolphins are slowly disappearing, and so are their river biomes.

HOME SWEET HOME

The pink river dolphin grows to 2.7 metres long. It swims with paddle-like flippers and uses **echolocation** in the muddy water to find prey, which it catches in its long slender beak. Sadly, many river dolphins have died due to pollution, becoming tangled in fishing gear or because noisy boats make it difficult for the dolphin to find food.

# Glossary

**adapted** Changed to survive in an environment.

**biomes** Communities of plants and animals living together in a certain kind of climate.

**breeding** Having young.

**camouflage** A colour or pattern that matches the surrounding environment and helps an organism to hide.

**conservation** The act of guarding, protecting or preserving something.

**digest** To break down food so it can be absorbed by the body.

**echolocation** The use of echoes to find things.

**endangered** When a plant or animal is in danger of dying out.

**gills** Body parts that fish and some other animals use to breathe underwater.

**hibernate** To go into a special long sleep to survive cold winters when there is little food to eat.

**larvae** Animals at the stage when they have just hatched out of eggs.

**mammals** Types of animals that feed their babies with milk from their bodies.

**migration** Movement from one place to another in different seasons.

**oxygen** A colourless gas in the air we breathe.

**photosynthesis** The process plants use to make their own food.

**pollution** Something harmful put into water, air or land.

**predator** An animal that catches and eats other animals.

**prey** An animal that is caught and eaten by other animals.

**roots** Plant parts that grow under the ground or water and take in water.

**scales** Small, overlapping plates of hard material.

**talons** Large curved claws on a bird's feet.

**territory** An area that an animal guards as its own.

**webbed** Having skin between toes or fingers.

# Further Reading

Jinny Johnson, *Watery Worlds: Rivers and Lakes*, Franklin Watts, 2015

Leon Gray, *Amazing Habitats: Rivers and Lakes*, Franklin Watts, 2015

*Rushing Rivers: Everything You Want to Know about Rivers Great and Small in One Amazing Book*, Kingfisher, 2016

Sean Callery, *River (Life Cycles)*, Kingfisher, 2013

Steve Parker, *Eyewitness Pond & River (DK Eyewitness Books)*, Dorling Kindersley, 2011

# Websites

Learn more about rivers and the animals that live in them at:
**www.bbc.co.uk/nature/habitats/River**

Explore animals that live in freshwater biomes at:
**http://a-z-animals.com/reference/freshwater**

Find out more about freshwater at:
**http://wwf.panda.org/about_our_earth/about_freshwater**

Discover more about threats to rivers and lakes at:
**http://wwf.panda.org/about_our_earth/about_freshwater/ freshwater_problems**

# Index